LET'S LEARN ABOUT FOOD

MEAT AND FISH

Samantha Nugent

LET'S READ
AV2 BY WEIGL
ADDED VALUE · AUDIO VISUAL

www.av2books.com

Go to **www.av2books.com**, and enter this book's unique code.

BOOK CODE

U 2 2 7 6 3 3

AV² by Weigl brings you media enhanced books that support active learning.

AV² provides enriched content that supplements and complements this book. Weigl's AV² books strive to create inspired learning and engage young minds in a total learning experience.

Your AV² Media Enhanced books come alive with...

Audio
Listen to sections of the book read aloud.

Video
Watch informative video clips.

Embedded Weblinks
Gain additional information for research.

Try This!
Complete activities and hands-on experiments.

Key Words
Study vocabulary, and complete a matching word activity.

Quizzes
Test your knowledge.

Slide Show
View images and captions, and prepare a presentation.

... and much, much more!

Published by AV² by Weigl
350 5th Avenue, 59th Floor
New York, NY 10118

Website: www.av2books.com

Library of Congress Control Number: 2015937778

ISBN 978-1-4896-3999-8 (hardcover)
ISBN 978-1-4896-4000-0 (soft cover)
ISBN 978-1-4896-4001-7 (single user eBook)
ISBN 978-1-4896-4002-4 (multi-user eBook)

Printed in the United States of America in Brainerd, Minnesota
1 2 3 4 5 6 7 8 9 0 19 18 17 16 15

062015
160615

Editor: Katie Gillespie   Designer: Mandy Christiansen

Weigl acknowledges Getty Images, iStock, and Shutterstock as the primary image suppliers for this title.

<figure>**2**</figure>

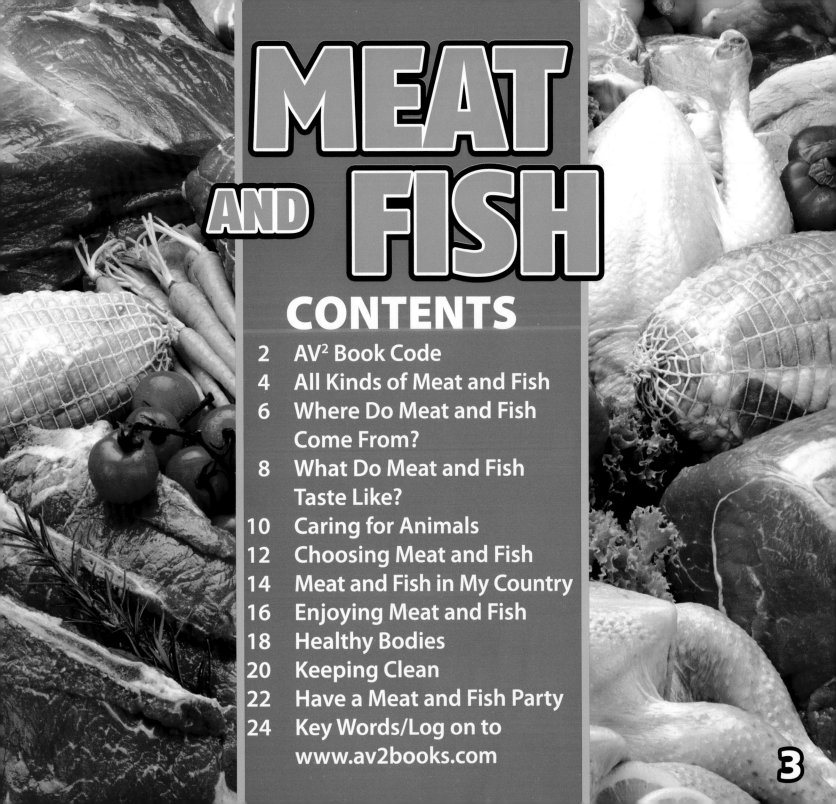

MEAT AND FISH

CONTENTS

I like to eat meat and fish. Meat and fish come in many different shapes, sizes, and colors.

5

Meat comes from animals, such as pigs and cows. These animals live on farms. Most fish comes from the ocean.

Chicken and pork are kinds of meat. Tuna and salmon are types of fish.

7

Meat and fish often feel chewy and soft. They have a special flavor. It is called umami.

I like to eat meat and fish at meals and at snack time. Sometimes, I eat dried meat or fish.

Farmers give their animals food, water, and shelter. This helps the animals stay healthy and happy.

A pen can help keep pigs safe.

11

Meat and fish must be cut and cleaned. Butchers help get meat and fish ready to eat.

I help choose my meat and fish at the grocery store and butcher shop. Sometimes, I choose meat and fish in cans.

13

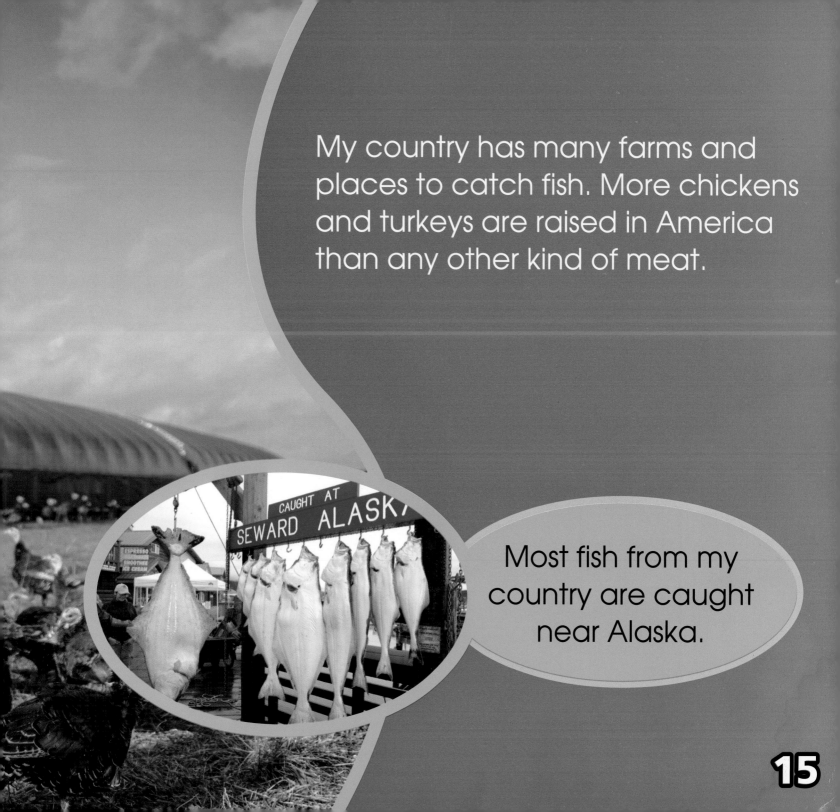

My country has many farms and places to catch fish. More chickens and turkeys are raised in America than any other kind of meat.

Most fish from my country are caught near Alaska.

Many foods have meat or fish in them. Cheeseburgers and sandwiches can both be made with meat.

I like to eat foods made with meat or fish.

Eating meat and fish
gives me energy to play.

I eat many kinds of
meat and fish to
stay healthy.

It is important to make sure my meat and fish are fresh. They stay fresh longer when they are stored in the refrigerator.

I wash my hands with soap and warm water before I eat. I sing *Happy Birthday* two times to make sure I have scrubbed long enough.

How to Make Tasty Tuna Sandwiches

Meat and fish are even better when you share them with your friends and family. Enjoy your tasty tuna sandwiches at lunch time. This recipe makes enough for four servings. Add any of your favorite cheeses or vegetables to this recipe.

You will need:

- an adult
- kitchen sink
- 1 dish towel
- 1 large spoon
- 1 large bowl
- 12 ounces (340 grams) of canned tuna
- 4 tablespoons (60 milliliters) of mayonnaise
- 2 tablespoons (30 ml) of relish
- 4 large leaves of lettuce
- 8 slices of whole grain bread

Directions

1. Wash your hands with soap and warm water.

2. Run the lettuce under cold water and dry it with a clean dish towel.

3. Have an adult help open the canned tuna and empty it into the large bowl.

4. Add the mayonnaise and relish to the bowl of tuna. Use the large spoon to mix the ingredients together.

5. Spread the tuna mixture evenly onto four pieces of bread. Add the lettuce on top of the tuna mixture.

6. Put one slice of bread on top of each sandwich.

7. Refrigerate any leftover tuna mixture.

8. Share your tasty tuna sandwiches with your friends and enjoy!

KEY WORDS

Research has shown that as much as 65 percent of all written material published in English is made up of 300 words. These 300 words cannot be taught using pictures or learned by sounding them out. They must be recognized by sight. This book contains 68 common sight words to help young readers improve their reading fluency and comprehension. This book also teaches young readers several important content words, such as proper nouns. These words are paired with pictures to aid in learning and improve understanding.

Page	Sight Words First Appearance
4	and, come, different, eat, I, in, like, many, to
7	animals, are, as, farms, from, kinds, live, most, of, on, such, the, these
8	a, at, have, is, it, often, or, sometimes, they, time
11	can, food, give, helps, keep, their, this, water
12	be, cut, get, must, my
15	America, any, country, has, more, near, other, places, than
16	both, made, them, with
19	me, play
20	before, enough, hands, important, long, make, two, when

Page	Content Words First Appearance
4	colors, fish, meat, shapes, sizes
7	chicken, cows, ocean, pigs, pork, salmon, tuna
8	meals, umami
11	farmers, pen, shelter
12	butchers, butcher shop, cans, grocery store
15	Alaska, turkeys
16	cheeseburgers, sandwiches
19	energy
20	*Happy Birthday*, refrigerator, soap

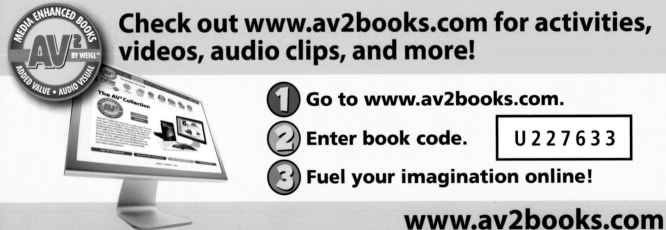

MEDIA ENHANCED BOOKS
AV²
BY WEIGL™
ADDED VALUE • AUDIO VISUAL

Check out www.av2books.com for activities, videos, audio clips, and more!

The AV² Collection

1. **Go to www.av2books.com.**
2. **Enter book code.** | U 2 2 7 6 3 3 |
3. **Fuel your imagination online!**

www.av2books.com